Breaking the Seattle Deadlock

Zhen Kun Wang
and L. Alan Winters

THE ROYAL INSTITUTE OF
INTERNATIONAL AFFAIRS
International Economics Programme

Published in Great Britain in 2000
by the Royal Institute of International Affairs,
Chatham House, 10 St James's Square, London SW1Y 4LE
(Charity Registration No. 208 223)

Distributed worldwide by the Brookings Institution,
1775 Massachusetts Avenue, NW, Washington, DC 20036-2188

ISBN 1 86203 118 5

Cover design by Matthew Link
Printed and bound in Great Britain by Chameleon Press Ltd

CONTENTS

FOREWORD

The obligation should always be 'for the academic scholars to break ranks, to cut through the fog of obfuscations that attends the politics of policy making, to call a spade a spade, to say 'Oh bunk!' when necessary, and to propose policies and advance agendas that reflection and analysis lead one to believe to be good and beneficial, even when they appear outlandish now and will bring one neglect, at best, and opprobrium, at worst' (Bhagwati, 1998, pp. xiv–xv).

This ideal shines through the work of Wang and Winters in this paper. Not only does their essay prospect for better policy, their search is based on well-informed and deep scholarship, which give it power and clarity. Trade policy, when not founded on thorough research or when too narrowly entangled with domestic policies, is beset by confusion (for example, the debate about child labour confuses issues of trade and development).

Thanks to the authors, we are shown a way out of the deadlock of Seattle, or rather ways of 'putting Humpty together again', as an earlier version of the paper was called. This essay demonstrates that free trade is not hampered by 'unfair' trading by developing countries as a result of their lower environmental and labour standards, but rather the opposite: that the danger comes from the developed world, which finds it convenient to regard any difference in labour and environmental standards as 'social dumping' and 'ecodumping'. At the same time, the developed countries do not seem very keen to respect any previous trade engagements or to engage in a real dialogue with countries that have a fundamentally different standard of living.

These mistaken approaches have the potential to undermine free trade and to recreate a divide between the North and the South, between the rich and the poor, and to deadlock all trade negotiations. It is to be hoped that international trade policy officials will heed the concrete and straightforward recommendations contained in this paper and help to ensure that trade negotiations resume at all levels.

Dr Brigitte Granville
Head, International Economics Programme
Royal Institute of International Affairs

ACKNOWLEDGMENTS

We are grateful to many colleagues for conversations on this subject, and to Richard Baldwin, Brigitte Granville and Stephen Yeo for comments on the previous draft. An earlier, significantly different, version of this paper was published in April 2000 by the Centre for Economic Policy Research, London as *Putting 'Humpty' Together Again: Including Developing Countries in a Consensus for the WTO* (Policy Paper 4).

May 2000

ZKW
LAW

ABOUT THE AUTHORS

Zhen Kun Wang is a Research Fellow in the International Economics Programme at the Royal Institute of International Affairs, London.

L. Alan Winters is Professor of Economics at the University of Sussex and a Research Fellow at the Centre for Economic Policy Research, London.

1 INTRODUCTION

Seattle was a mess. The failure of the Ministerial meeting in December 1999 to initiate a new round of world trade talks was a blow to those of us who see trade liberalization as an important component of economic management and development. It represented a severe setback for hopes of harnessing the trading system as a stimulus for economic growth. The failure stemmed from a variety of causes including the WTO members' widely disparate positions and interests on most issues; the generally lukewarm attitude of governments towards trade liberalization; and a failure of the governance of the WTO as an institution. The high level of trust that is necessary to span the large differences in attitudes and interests characteristic of trade negotiations was completely absent. The fractures ran in several directions, the most severe being that between the developing and the developed countries. The former felt completely excluded from the process in Seattle, both procedurally and because they were unable to make their voices heard in the substantive debates and preparations.

Many policy-makers have expressed a welcome determination to get the 'WTO show' back on the road. High on the list of their priorities for repairing the damage done at Seattle must be to cement the developing countries more securely in to the trading system. After all, developing countries comprise a large majority of the WTO membership and account for an increasing share of world trade and the bulk of its growth. They feel frustrated over the implementation of the Uruguay Round agreements and the unsympathetic attitude of the developed countries towards their aspirations for the trading system. They were reluctant to contemplate a new Round, and Seattle made it worse. Now, it becomes both more challenging and more important to bring them actively into the coalition to preserve the trading system and to build confidence in the WTO.

Seattle revealed starkly the narrow self-interest that motivated the developed countries which, having once missed an existing opportunity to strike a bargain, will find it more expensive to construct a new one. The fabric of the system has been torn, and it will be impossible to put it together again without the active commitment and enthusiasm of the majority of its members. Rebuilding the legitimacy of the world trading system in the eyes of the majority of its members is not a matter of charity or development assistance, rather a matter of self-interest for the developed world, which still has much to gain from both the further liberalization of world trade and the disciplines that an effective WTO imposes on domestic discretion. The main contribution of the GATT (now WTO) system was to fortify governments against the narrow and sectoral interests of their domestic pressure groups. Any observer of the way the European Union kowtowed to its farm groups or the US government to its labour groups would conclude that this medicine is as much required in rich as in poor countries.

All in all, developed and developing countries alike need a rule-based world trading system, and they will all benefit from another round of trade liberalization. An effective coalition for the trading system has to be put back together before any talks are started to initiate such a round. In terms of the developing/developed-country fracture line, we argue, this will require greater attention to both the substantive needs of developing countries and procedural reform of the WTO. The latter is required to ensure that developing countries are no longer excluded from negotiations either formally, as (unforgivably) happened in Seattle, or informally through lack of a voice in Geneva. The developed countries, particularly the major players – the United States, the EU and Japan – also need to review and revise the widely disparate agendas that they took to the Seattle, and to start to bridge their differences.

We believe it is now even more crucial that any forthcoming round of trade talks must be a

'Development Round'. For such a round to be plausible in the current circumstances, however, real concessions from the developed world are required. We also argue that the best strategy for developing countries is not to resist a new round and liberalization, but to embrace them and focus them on those countries' development needs. They should approach the WTO negotiations with a firm view of their development priorities, and seek to ensure that WTO obligations will assist in achieving them. The elements of our proposal for breaking the Seattle deadlock are summarized in the box.

Further liberalization

Agriculture

- Slash bound tariffs
- Ban export subsidies
- Abolish subsidies that boost farm output

Manufactures

- Reduce bound tariffs, especially in developing countries
- Eliminate tariff escalation and remove tariff peaks, especially in developed countries

Services

- Enhance access for foreign services suppliers to developing-country markets
- Liberalize domestic regulations in developing countries to encourage competition and enhance social goals

- Liberalize the movement of 'natural persons', especially to allow developing-country workers temporary entry to developed-country service markets

Give credit for developing countries' unilateral trade liberalization

Reinvent special and differential treatment for the 21st century

- Judge rules changes against a development yardstick
- Allow greater procedural flexibility for developing countries

Make promises of technical assistance legally binding

- Developing countries should not sign any agreement until their requirements for implementing the agreement are known and resources for the implementation recognized and committed
- Technical assistance is not a one-off event but rather a long-term commitment

Honour the agreement on phasing-out of the MFA

- Ensure textiles and clothing trade fall completely under the GATT disciplines

- Allow only extremely limited use of safeguards on textile and clothing trade

What should not be on the agenda

- Shift issues of labour standards into the International Labour Organization
- Permit environmental trade policy *only* when multilaterally sanctioned by an appropriate multilateral environmental agreement
- Drop investment and competition policy off the agenda for now

Bridge the differences between the USA and the EU

- Review and revise the agenda taken to the Seattle
- Make publicly the firm commitments to the multilateral trade liberalization and rule-based world trading system

Improve the governance of the WTO

- Strengthen developing countries' capacity to deal with trade and WTO
- Streamline WTO governance to facilitate pre-negotiation discussions but recognize that consensus is the only basis for binding agreements

2 FURTHER LIBERALIZATION OF TRADE IN AGRICULTURE, MANUFACTURES AND SERVICES

2.1 Agriculture

The Uruguay Round made good progress in bringing agriculture under regular GATT disciplines (Martin and Winters 1996). The next round must continue the process by removing the remaining non-tariff barriers unique to agriculture and then liberalizing trade by reducing tariffs. At present, barriers to trade in agricultural products are several times higher than barriers to trade in manufactures. Figure 1 shows that the OECD estimates total levels of support at 18% of the value of output in the USA, 66% in the EU, and an outrageous 252% and 283% in Norway and Switzerland respectively (Anderson, Erwidodo and Ingco 1999). Compared with manufactures, the shares of agriculture in total world trade and production are much smaller, yet the cost of agricultural protection to the world economy roughly equals that of manufactures. For most farm products and countries, actual tariffs provide no less protection than did the non-tariff import barriers of the late 1980s/early 1990s. Tariffication of agricultural trade in the Uruguay Round made restrictions to imports more transparent, but the degree of 'water' currently in those tariffs makes most bindings ineffective. Binding tariffs at such a high level allows countries to vary their actual protection as they wish in response to changes in domestic and international food markets. This means that there has been little or none of the reduction in fluctuations in international food markets that tariffication was expected to deliver. Reducing bound tariffs from their current 50–150% to the 0–15% range that characterizes manufactures is one of the major challenges and potential benefits ahead.

Several non-tariff barriers are unique to agricultural trade, e.g. tariff-rate quotas, export subsidies and various forms of domestic support measures. The 'tariff-rate quotas' apply when countries reduce the tariffs charged on a given level of their imports of various commodities in order to guarantee a negotiated minimum level of import penetration. In fact the allocation of these (low-tariff) quotas across suppliers is arbitrary and biased. It results in inefficiency (high-cost suppliers got the quotas), favouritism, political pressures and, sometimes, under-shooting the minimum because the quotas go to countries that cannot supply. It is estimated that rents from tariff-rate quotas on agricultural imports to OECD countries amount to $25 billion per year based on 1996 international prices (Elbehri et al. 1999). Expanding tariff rate quotas – i.e. the quantity of imports permitted at low tariff rates – will reduce their importance, increase competition and lessen the impact of the excessively high above-quota tariffs.

Export subsidies undercut local producers in developing countries but are not much help to consumers because they are unreliable and likely to disappear as soon as world prices rise. Nothing less than a ban on agricultural export subsidies is needed, bringing agriculture into line with non-farm products under the GATT.

A whole raft of domestic support measures expands agricultural output in developed countries (generally the less efficient producers), wasting resources there and undermining efficient production and income generation in developing countries. For both efficiency and equity, the general level of domestic support needs to fall further. The so-called 'blue box' – a set of subsidy policies permitted by the Uruguay Round even though they were known to boost farm output – needs to be abolished. The criteria for the 'green box' (for subsidies that do not affect output) ought to be tightened up in order to reduce the number of loopholes that currently still permit output-increasing subsidies.

Agricultural liberalization is predominantly a job for developed countries – particularly the EU and Japan, which went to great lengths in Seattle to shift the focus elsewhere by enlarging the agenda. If achieved, developing-country suppliers of temperate products will see large export (and income) increases, and there will probably be some spillovers to tropical products. Agricultural growth strongly favours the poor and so the benefits will flow to where they are most needed (see, for example, Ravallion and Datt (1996). World prices of agricultural products will probably rise with liberalization, but this is not likely to be a major problem even for net food-importing developing countries. First, the increases are likely to be only a few percentage points, compared with regular fluctuations measured in tens of percentage points. Second, many developing countries currently import food only because of their own distortionary policies. Protection in the manufacturing and services sectors bestows a significant anti-agriculture bias in many low- and medium-income countries, making it more difficult for them to benefit from the agricultural trade reform in developed countries. For such countries economic theory shows that, even though the prices of their imports rise, world food price rises make them better off (Tyers and Falvey 1989): they are initially losing welfare by unnecessarily stimulating food imports, and the price rise curtails that stimulus.

Developing countries have a significant stake in the process of farm policy reform. One simple model of the world economy suggests that a reduction of 40% in the barriers to world farm trade will generate economic gains of at least $15 billion per

Figure 1: Agricultural support in the OECD, 1997

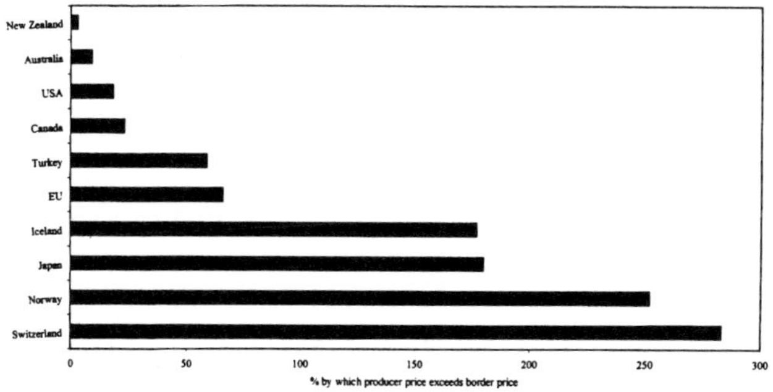

Source: Anderson, Erwidodo and Ingco (1999), Table 2.

year by 2005[1] (Hertel et al. 1999). OECD countries are estimated to gain about $55 billion per year from the same liberalization – greater than developing countries' gains because it is mainly developed-country inefficiencies that are removed by the

[1] These results (and all the other forecasts of the effects of future rounds) are based on computable general equilibrium models. Their absolute sizes should not be taken too seriously, and it should always be remembered that they reflect their authors' assumptions and approximations. However, provided these exercises are carefully conducted and honestly reported, their results are useful in suggesting the *relative* importance of different policies and highlighting broad issues.

reduction in barriers. Other estimates are of substantially higher gains for developing countries, which seems plausible given the difficulties of capturing all the complexities of agricultural policy and the extremely high rates of protection that particular agricultural products receive.

2.2 Manufactures

The share of manufactures in developing-country exports has increased dramatically, from around 30% in early 1980 to over 70% in 1995, and probably approaching 80% by 2005 (Hertel and Martin 1999). Manufactures trade between developing countries has also been increasing steadily over time. About 40% of developing-country exports of manufactures went to other developing countries in 1995.

Figure 2 shows that developed-country tariffs on manufactured imports are quite low on average (1.5%), but that they impinge more heavily on exports from the developing world (3.4%) than on those from other developed countries (0.8%). Moreover, within the average there are both peaks of 15%, 20% or 25% on goods in which developing countries are competitive, and significant escalation. Escalation means that tariffs rise with the degree of processing, which makes it more difficult for developing countries to export processed goods. There are some significant areas such as steel, leather, footwear, textiles and clothing

Figure 2: Average tariffs on developed- and developing-country exports of manufactures

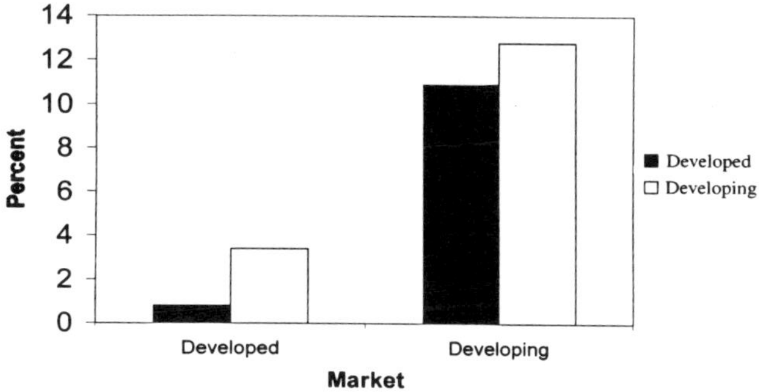

Source: Derived from Hertel and Martin (1999).

in which developing countries can benefit from important concessions from developed ones.

Much more important, however, are developing countries' own barriers to manufactures. These average tariffs of 10.9% on developed countries' manufactured exports and 12.8% on developing countries' (Figure 2). Liberalizing these will have immediate consumer gains in developing countries and longer-term efficiency benefits as industry adjusts. It will stimulate growth in trade between developing countries and also, in the present context, provide specie with which to 'buy' other concessions from developed countries in the negotiations.

Developing countries stand to make substantial gains from further liberalizing manufactures trade

– much larger, in fact, than those accruing to developed countries ($52 billion as opposed to $18 billion per year from a 40% reduction in barriers). This imbalance reflects a combination of the facts that, facing higher tariffs to start with, developing countries achieve larger absolute improvements in access to export markets and that, starting with much higher tariffs of their own, developing countries obtain much greater efficiency gains from a given proportionate liberalization (Hertel et al. 1999).

2.3 Services

The service sector is far larger than manufacturing or agriculture, and almost certainly more protected (Hoekman 1996). Developing countries have been reluctant to liberalize services, fearing that they have nothing to gain. This is wrong. As they are importers, a supply of reliable and cheap business services would aid efficiency in all sectors of their economies, while consumers would stand to gain from liberalization of some other services. Moreover, importing services or allowing foreign firms to establish themselves in these countries' home markets is quite consistent with prudential or quality regulation.[2] However, liberalizing foreign

[2] Liberalizing the provision of banking services is *not* the same thing as liberalizing capital flows. Foreign-owned banks can be made subject to the same supervisory and precautionary regulations as domestic banks, but they might still be much more efficient at delivering services.

supply is not sufficient. Developing countries need also to liberalize domestic services markets at the same time. This should entail improved rules and domestic regulations – first, to encourage economic efficiency by remedying market failures; and, second, to pursue social goals (Mattoo 1999).

Policy-makers should emphasize competition rather than ownership when negotiating services markets because larger welfare gains arise from increased competition than simply from changes of ownership: increased competition brings benefits through both allocative and internal efficiency. Liberalizing imported services markets by eliminating explicit trade restrictions and implicit regulatory barriers to foreign services can strongly increase effective competition, and this is clearly business for a round of trade talks. But reforming the regulations governing domestic firms can often go further, and this move too can be aided by placing it an international context. Developing countries should use strengthened multilateral disciplines on domestic regulations to promote and consolidate domestic reform, as they did in telecommunications over the 1990s. Also, such disciplines give developing-country exporters the means to address regulatory barriers to their exports in foreign markets.

However, there are limits to what can be achieved at the multilateral level: multilateral trade rules are designed to ensure market access, rather than directly to promote competition. Thus in parallel with any trade talks developing countries should strengthen their purely domestic rules to encourage economic efficiency in remedying market failure and pursuing social goals.

Developing countries also have as much to gain as exporters of services, particularly with regard to the temporary movement of natural persons to supply services in a foreign market. Under the General Agreement on Trade in Services (GATS) – negotiated in the Uruguay Round – the liberalization commitments were very limited in this area. Of the four modes of supply recognized by the GATS – cross-border supply, consumption abroad, commercial presence (i.e. foreign direct investment) and presence of natural persons – the last attracted the fewest commitments. Those that were made were of very limited sectoral coverage and were conditional on factors such as the length of stay, the state of the labour market and the 'economic need' for imports. Even where commitments were made to freeze existing regulations, the latter are so obscure that it is unclear what has been gained (Chanda 1999).

Almost inevitably, the least liberal commitments (or the complete absence of commitments) are in sectors or areas where developing countries have a comparative advantage, i.e., in low- and medium-skill-related labour-intensive activities. The commitments that have been made generally have only limited significance for developing countries because they refer almost exclusively to higher-level personnel who are typically associated with commercial presence in capital-intensive activities. If the GATS is to promote trade in services and address the interests of developing countries effectively, the industrial countries must negotiate *in good faith* in this key area of the 'movement of natural persons'.

Four classes of continuing constraints on the movement of natural persons need to be negotiated. They include:

- immigration-related regulations concerning the entry and stay of service providers;
- regulations concerning the recognition of qualifications, work experience and training;
- differential treatment of domestic and foreign personnel;
- regulations covering other modes of supply, particularly commercial presence, which indirectly limit the scope for the movement of natural persons.

The fundamental problem is that there is no separation between temporary and permanent labour movement, even though GATS is meant to cover only temporary labour flows in services. At present, the temporary movement of labour comes under the purview of immigration legislation and labour market conditions. In a new round it will be important to separate temporary from permanent movement of labour and provide suitable provision for *short-term* mobility of workers. The multilateral discussions should also aim at sector-specific commitments, especially in sectors such as professional and business services, and on expanding the categories of service providers to remove the current bias towards higher-level personnel. It is important to include middle- and low-skill-level providers and make the commitments more relevant to the interests of developing countries with capacity in these categories (Chanda 1999).

All in all, with suitable provision for *short-term* mobility of workers (not migration), developing countries could greatly expand the supply of services to developed-country consumers and businesses. With greater liberalization, many more developing countries could export services such as construction, distribution, environment and transport. The current success stories of developing countries exporting services, such as Indian software or Cuban health services, rely significantly on provider mobility. Indian software exports grew from US $225 million in 1992–3 to US $1.75 billion in 1997–8 and may reach, as reported in the *Financial Times* on 7 February 2000, US $6.32 billion in 2000–01. Despite the growing importance of cross-border electronic delivery, the movement of natural persons remains a critical part of the equation. In the early 1990s, the US government introduced rules that obliged foreign workers to acquire temporary work visas (H1-B visas). The number of visas issued during a year was limited to 65,000. In 1998, in response to mounting labour shortages experienced in the information and technology sector, the United States relaxed its temporary visa requirements for skilled workers and the annual visa cap was raised to 115,000 for both 1999 and 2000. This shows the sort of advantages that developed-country producers perceive in relaxing the movement of natural persons and suggests the sort of allies that developing countries could find in pursuing this issue (Mattoo 1999).

It is premature to talk of numbers, but preliminary estimates suggest large potential gains from 'ordinary' trade liberalization like this. One set of estimates (Hertel et al. 1999) suggests that, by reducing world trade barriers by 40% in 2005, developing and developed countries will gain roughly $180 billion and $320 billion respectively. One should certainly not take these figures literally, but they are an indication that there are still significant benefits to be reaped through simple trade liberalization. Trade policy reform mainly benefits the countries that undertake it rather than their partners.

3 CREDIT FOR UNILATERAL LIBERALIZATION

Many developing countries have liberalized their trade unilaterally since the end of the Uruguay Round, frequently lowering applied tariffs well below the rates they agreed ('bound' in WTO-speak) in the Round. They fear that such reductions will erode their bargaining power in any forthcoming talks (Croome 1998). Developed countries must reassure them that this is not so. They must treat reductions in bound rates, which are the subject of WTO negotiations, as concessions to be reciprocated, even if the bindings do not come down to the rates actually applied and hence do not imply an immediate reduction in the tariffs charged on the ground.

Reductions in bound rates are valuable even if they do not immediately lower applied rates because they remove uncertainty: they lower the maximum legal tariff (Martin and Francois 1994). Besides, by offering credit, developed countries will help to foster further unilateral liberalization, which, in the past, has benefited them as well as the developing countries undertaking it. For their own sakes developing countries should use credit not to avoid making cuts in actual tariffs, but as a means of encouraging deeper liberalization in the developed world. If they do this, making provision for credit in the Round would be both equitable and constructive as well as a useful gesture towards developing countries.

4 CREATING 21ST-CENTURY 'SPECIAL AND DIFFERENTIAL' TREATMENT

'Special and differential treatment' referred to GATT/WTO rights and privileges given to developing countries, but not extended to developed countries. It covered both special rights for developing countries to protect their domestic markets and producers, and special market access (tariff preferences) for their exports to developed-country markets. In the 1980s intellectual opinion on economic development shifted away from import substitution and many developing countries started unilateral trade liberalization. The Uruguay Round agreements reduced the scope of special and differential treatment, but did not completely eliminate it. Instead, they focused it on the adjustment and implementation capacity problems facing developing countries (Whalley 1999).

Despite special and differential treatment, developing countries felt overburdened with implementing the Uruguay Round agreements and insisted that, if there were a new round, they be exempt from much of its likely liberalization and new rules. In effect they were looking back towards the special and differential treatment of the past, which had tended to deflect them from trade liberalization and which, as a result, left them largely outside the GATT system and, frequently, outside the huge increase in prosperity that it engendered.

Special and differential treatment has not been a constructive force in the past. Letting developing-countries off the liberalization of their own barriers undermined liberal forces at home and left developing-country negotiators nothing to negotiate with in the rounds (Finger 1991). Neither have the preferences which developing countries have fought so hard to preserve been a success overall (Wang and Winters 1997, Whalley 1999). Under the General System of Preferences (GSP) or, for the EU, the Lomé Convention for African, Caribbean and Pacific (ACP) countries, industrial countries grant preferential tariffs to developing countries' exports. In most goods the margins of tariff preference are small because tariffs are low in industrial countries. Where they are not small, the preferences are constrained either quantitatively or by stringent rules of origin and a threat of graduation (i.e. that the exporter has become too competitive to be treated specially). The complicated procedures of the rules of origin cost exporters from poor country dearly in terms of paperwork. In certain areas where developing countries have comparative advantage they may have no preferences at all – e.g. the USA's GSP excludes clothing.

In the few cases where preference margins are material, they are no basis for investment and development because they are insecure. As we argued above, conditions such as rules of origin, eligibility, renewal and graduation attached to all GSP schemes create uncertainty for long-term investment. Preferences teach developing-country negotiators to focus on short-term quasi-rents (i.e. pocketing the revenue from the tariffs they have been let off while the concession lasts) rather than to focus on the long-term needs of assured access for commercially viable products. It also opens them up to pressure on unrelated issues such as labour standards. It is in the best interest of developing countries that they stick with the basic rules of trade liberalization – non-discrimination (most favoured nation and national treatment), binding tariffs in all sectors and cutting 'bound' tariffs through negotiations.

However, there is still scope for a new form of special and differential treatment, which enhances effective liberalization rather than impeding it. This would recognize the genuine differences in institutions and objectives between developed and developing countries and tailor liberalization and new regulations to these differences. Thus, for example, if future trade talks introduce measures that require more difficult or more costly transitions for developing countries, these should be recognized in terms of longer periods, more flexible rules and specific offers of technical assistance. To prevent longer transition periods from being used merely to put off adjustment, however, developing countries should agree to phased transitions with monitorable mileposts, so that both the international community *and their own citizens* can see that adjustment is actually occurring.

Special and differential treatment might also be extended to some rule changes on a more permanent basis. The Uruguay Round agreements include commitments to modernize trade procedures such as import licensing and customs valuation, and to reform areas of regulation which relate to domestic business environment. As Finger and Hoekman (1999) argue, given the disparities in negotiating power and resources, negotiations on rules tend to reflect the agenda of rich countries and their specific interest groups. Therefore, the existing WTO rules are in large part a codification of the rules and institutions in developed countries. They work well there, but not necessarily in poor countries.

In some cases the requirements of the WTO agreements, while not harmful *per se*, are not well suited to developing countries' development objectives. One example is the Customs Valuation Agreement. Valuation is only one part of the customs process. Given the initially weak situation in many developing countries, changing the valuation method without overall customs reform is not likely to improve the predictability of the customs process, nor to mitigate significantly the possibility of using the customs process as a non-tariff barrier. For example, nearly all developing countries face difficulties over customs administration, but inappropriate valuation methods rank far behind factors such as corruption, lack of codification and mechanization, and unreliable timing. Thus the WTO Customs Valuation Agreement, which prescribes how imports are to be valued, is more or less irrelevant for many developing countries. A global regime more sympathetic to an honest and verifiable reference price system (which is banned under the Uruguay Round Agreement) would be better. It would leave more developing-country resources and effort over for reforms that are more important. Finger and Schuler (1999) characterize the Customs Valuation Agreement as addressing only a small proportion of developing countries' customs problems, providing no remedy for the remainder and being inappropriate in the areas it does cover.

In future rule changes should be judged against a development yardstick. Many reforms would pass the test and apply to all WTO members, but others would need to be modified for poor countries. In many of the new negotiating areas on domestic regulation and institutions, there is no developing-country trial and error experience from which to infer the development implications of multilateral rules. WTO rules should allow for such experimentation and learning. Creating such flexibility, while at the same time preserving predictability and transparency for traders, would be a useful form of special and differential treatment for developing countries in the next round. One approach might be to allow greater (although not complete) procedural flexibility, while requiring that outcomes be fair. Criteria for assessing the fairness of outcomes and procedures without overburdening the dispute settlement process would need to be developed. Perhaps, for example, the right to use unorthodox procedures could be made conditional upon agreeing to a fast-track administrative review of contentious policies.

Rule-mandated reform will cost money and many developing countries will need extra funding and technical assistance (see section 5). However, the question of where to spend the limited resources deserves attention. If the development dimension is absent in the rules, money spent on implementing them might be wasted. For example, an extra dollar spent on health care or education in most poor countries might be more appropriate and more productive than spending it on implementing intellectual property rules.

5 LEGALLY BINDING TECHNICAL ASSISTANCE

For the many new areas of regulation introduced in the Uruguay Round, effective implementation and compliance involve heavy investment. For example, the introduction of legislation, the creation of administrative bodies, staff training, equipment and buildings all cost money. Finger and Schuler (1999) estimate that it costs, on average, $130–150 million per country to meet the WTO rules in just three areas – intellectual property, sanitary and phytosanitary standards and customs valuation. This sum exceeds an entire year's development budget in many of the least developed countries.

The Uruguay Round agreements are replete with promises of technical assistance to developing countries to help them undertake the agreed reforms, but most of these promises were not binding and many have not been delivered. Since the developing countries clearly saw such assistance as a quid pro quo for certain agreements or concessions, this is hardly fair. Neither is it efficient. Given their limited human resources and institutional capacity, many developing countries, particular the poor and small ones, have significant difficulties implementing the agreements and integrating themselves into the world trading system. Solving these difficulties is likely to benefit both the countries themselves and their trading partners. The next round needs to find a means of making promises of technical assistance binding – i.e. justiciable and subject to complaint/retaliation. One solution might be to establish a fund from which developing countries were entitled to draw agreed amounts. The Trade and Development Committee of the WTO might be authorized to manage the fund.

Ensuring effective use of resources requires the establishment of a well-designed and functioning mechanism. The current model, the Integrated Framework,[3] may form a suitable basis, although, in truth, it has several shortcomings. It involves six international agencies – WTO, IMF, World Bank, International Trade Centre (ITC), United Nations Conference on Trade and Development (UNCTAD) and United Nations Development Programme (UNDP). It aims at improving the overall capacity of the least developed countries to respond to the challenges and opportunities offered by the world trading system. It provides trade-related technical assistance, including human and institutional capacity-building to handle trade policy issues and strengthen export supply capabilities. Involving

[3] This was developed in 1997 as part of the High-Level Meeting on Integrated Initiatives for the Least Developed Countries' Trade and Development (for more detail see *www.idcs.org*).

international development agencies such as the World Bank and UNCTAD helps to ensure that each participating country defines its trade-related assistance priorities according to its general development strategy. Given their world-wide experience in economic development, these international development agencies can play a crucial role in setting the agenda for the assistance plan and can help the least developed countries' governments to rank their trade-related technical assistance needs according to development priorities.

The process of the Integrated Framework begins with the identification of needs by each country, followed by a joint response to those needs by participating agencies. Each country develops its own integrated assistance plan. The Integrated Framework seems a sound approach – demand-driven, avoiding overlap among international organizations. The effectiveness of the Integrated Framework, however, depends on the quality of the need assessments at the start, of the follow-up and coordination among the participating international agencies, and of the resources available to meet these needs. In fact, all these aspects are causes for concern, especially the last, given that no new resources were earmarked for the programme. Unlike project financing, the very nature of much technical assistance – less money involved, but long time processes and a less visible and less immediate outcome – means it is desirable to design and implement a long-lasting, not a one-off programme. New resources, although not large in total, need to be kept trickling in continuously in order to keep the programme rolling. In particular, many technical assistance programmes cannot be fully assessed until they have operated for a long time. This calls for careful design with monitorable *process goals*, but it also calls for patience (and faith) in waiting for measurable outputs. The frequent changes in fashion observed in some international organizations and national administrations pose a serious danger to effective technical assistance. A key component of effective technical assistance is capacity-building: equipping developing countries not only to install, but to operate and develop necessary systems and institutions. The training element of such programmes is prolonged and, since staff trained effectively to operate complex public functions are likely to be very attractive to the private sector, constant replenishment is necessary. Such 'defection' is good news for the economy as it is probably the main route for the diffusion of skills and knowledge. However, it makes the continued operation of the public function at acceptable (and previously agreed) levels burdensome for many years.

The European Commission has suggested that, when an agreement is being concluded in the WTO, it should be accompanied by a framework to support its implementation in the light of country-specific requirements. The Commission argues that as technical assistance needs are so country-specific, technical assistance requirements should not be laid down in the agreement itself, but somehow 'identified in relation to the agreement'. We agree that developing countries clearly should not sign any agreement until their requirements for implementing the agreement are known. But we would also argue that if they need assistance to make implementation possible or desirable, they should not sign until these needs are recognized and the resources to meet them have been identified and guaranteed. Overall, the message here is clear. As other negotiated commitments are binding, technical assistance commitments should be binding too.

6 HONOUR THE AGREEMENT ON PHASING OUT THE MULTI-FIBRE AGREEMENT

The Uruguay Round agreed to phase out the quantitative restrictions on textile and clothing trade by the end of 2004. The liberalization was hugely end-loaded. Given developed countries' poor record in liberalizing this sector in the past, and given China's likely accession to the WTO by then, doubts about effective liberalization are legitimate. There are even rumours of plans for mass anti-dumping or safeguards actions in 2005. This would be a massive, and wholly unacceptable, breach of faith. Ideally the developed countries should pre-empt such worries by making public commitments that such a situation will not occur. In the meantime, developing countries need to make plain that there will be no settlement to the next round if the textiles and clothing agreement is not implemented in good faith. The intention, floated in Seattle, of a three-year round was never very plausible, but developing countries have a clear interest in postponing its conclusion until well into 2005, when the Multi-Fibre Agreement (MFA) quotas will all have been removed for some time.

7 WHAT SHOULD NOT BE ON THE AGENDA FOR THIS ROUND OF NEGOTIATIONS?

The fear that labour and environmental clauses in the WTO would foster protectionism is well grounded: think how anti-dumping has been abused. Moreover, if the WTO legitimized trade sanctions for social or environmental reasons, the WTO Appellate Body could become *de facto* the final arbiter of such standards. This seems both undesirable *per se*, and potentially so divisive that the WTO's traditional role in fostering trade could be undermined (Rollo and Winters 2000).

Developing countries are right to resist these additions to the WTO competence, absolutely for labour standards and nearly absolutely for the environment. If they have to give ground on the latter, it should only be to consider multilateral sanctions for breaches of multilateral environmental agreements where the breaches have been identified by a large majority of the countries in the world. One of the complications is that the some countries are members of the WTO, but are not the signatory countries of environmental agreements. Efforts should be made to encourage all countries to sign sensible environmental agreements that protect the global environment and enhance sustainable economic development in rich and poor countries alike. Without such efforts, unilateral trade sanctions by the rich countries against the poor ones, or threatening trade sanctions under the WTO, cannot reach the root of the problem.

Raising labour standards and increasing workers' wellbeing worldwide is the concern of everybody, not just of labour unions in the United States or other rich countries. However, using trade sanctions and trade protection will potentially add competitive advantages to the workers in rich countries. At the same time, it threatens to undermine the competitive position of workers in poor countries and to harm their interests, which the reputable developed-country labour unions are supposed to care for as well.

One of the main reasons for the Seattle collapse was President Clinton's call for labour standards with trade sanctions to be inserted into the WTO. Such a proposal is understandable given that the Democratic Party was seeking the support of labour unions for the presidential election. But it beggars belief that the president of the biggest player in the world trading system raised such a divisive issue in such a cynical and insensitive manner. Seattle failed and everybody went home. But the issue of labour standards will not go away. It may be more constructive for developing countries and supportive international organizations such as UNCTAD and the World Bank to invite their developed-country partners to discuss the issue, to explore the possibilities of using non-trade instruments in the International Labour Organization (ILO). This is a far more appropriate forum for a labour debate than the WTO. The ILO's lack of enforcement mechanism and capability has made it less attractive than the WTO to developed countries, but the agenda can include discussions on enforcement. Moreover, the ILO's traditional mechanism of naming and shaming transgressors has become far more in effective with the advent of the internet and the increased influence and organizational ability of the NGOs.

Here let us stress our position again. We, like most of the general public, are concerned about environment, health, social standards and cultural diversity, and recognize that globalization may affect all of these. But we also believe that solutions and instruments other than trade sanctions or trade instruments are required. We also believe that, whatever the solutions and approaches will be, they must be well balanced between the wishes of civil society in developed countries and the interests of developing countries.

There is no stomach for an investment negotiation so soon after the demise of the OECD's Multilateral Agreement on Investment (MAI). The factors that led to the abandonment of the MAI have not disappeared. The differences between OECD members that prevented an agreed final version of MAI have not been bridged (see Henderson 1999 for an excellent analysis). Moreover, liberalization of capital flows in general, and foreign direct investment (FDI) in particular, has been going on in many developing countries regardless of the OECD machinations.

On competition policy, the chances of a successful negotiation look no better. The difference of opinion between the EU and the US about whether competition policy should be included on the agenda is well known. How quickly the difference can be bridged is an open question, given the very different approaches that the parties adopt to competition at home. On top of that, what developing countries do not need is an obligation to create complex competition authorities: they will typically not have the resources either to create or to run them. If such organizations are to be legitimate and operate effectively they must emerge from concerns about domestic consumers, not from international concerns about market access (Hoekman and Holmes 1999). Developing countries might usefully seek means to manage international collusion and to control anti-dumping actions, which are, ostensibly, about predatory competition. On collusion, they might extract agreement that firms' (developed) home governments would act against export market power (a sort of positive comity). On anti-dumping, the need is for substantive reform but not greater procedural complexity. It must curb both developed and developing countries' activities.

Not only are investment policy and competition policy likely to yield little concrete progress in the next few years, but they could derail a new round. They will certainly be contentious and they will divert political and bureaucratic attention from the more straightforward and rewarding business of trade liberalization. Comprehensive rounds are desirable in that they increase the opportunities for trade-offs, but in the aftermath of Seattle it seems better to keep the agenda within fairly tight bounds in order to reach a consensus and not to overburden developing-country administrations with threatening and complex issues.

8 BRIDGE THE DIFFERENCES BETWEEN THE US AND THE EU

The transatlantic trade disputes over the issues of bananas, hormone-treated beef, tax treatment for Foreign Sales Corporations (FSCs) and genetically modified foods have hardly facilitated compromise between the US and the EU over what should be included in the Seattle discussions. It is beyond the scope of this paper to discuss these disputes. But it is plain that the cause of a future round of liberalization, not to mention the stability of the current system, will be immensely helped by a genuine willingness to settle them. Seattle has perhaps sounded a warning bell, for the rhetoric has moderated since the new year, but it will require serious political commitment to get these disputes resolved in the near future. For as long as they remain active they undermine the WTO and colour everyone else's perception of the major players' willingness to respect the system of which they often appear to be custodians.

Perhaps the major bone of contention between developed countries is agriculture. The EU and Japan, facing mounting pressure from domestic farmers, proposed the idea of 'multifunctionality of agriculture' and insisted on a 'comprehensive round' agenda. The US and other agricultural exporting countries saw this as a smokescreen to hide the reluctance of both the EU and Japan to tackle the fundamental problems of their agricultural sectors.

In trying to build up a consensus around a comprehensive round, the EU made a number of very sweeping promises to other countries – including adding all the 'so-called' implementation issues of the Uruguay Round to the agenda. This amounted in US eyes almost to tearing up the Uruguay Round, for on virtually every issue at least one country is claiming difficulties and wanting to be released from its commitments. Unwilling to countenance such revisionism, the US adopted a very hostile attitude towards the EU plan. If talks are to be revived, the US and EU must have a much closer conception of what is desirable and possible. The US 'market access plus labour standards' agenda did not win much applause in Seattle either. It seemed narrowly self-serving and, as we saw above, highly threatening to developing countries.

Both the US 'market access plus labour standards' agenda and the EU/Japanese 'everything but the kitchen sink' agenda reflected fundamentally commercial and domestic political considerations. All parties have to review and revise these positions. Pascal Lamy, in his speech to the European Parliament in Brussels on 25 January 2000, pointed out that 'we should not allow the institution [WTO] to become a scapegoat for our real differences on the substance and the lack of a political will to overcome these differences'.[4] The leaders from the both sides of the transatlantic relationship and from Japan have to confront their interest groups and work harder to bridge their differences. They should also once again show their firm commitment to multilateral trade liberalization and the rules-based world trading system under the WTO. It is, after all, the only one they have got.

[4] For the full text of his speech, see *http://europa.eu.int/comm/trade/2000-round*.

9 THE GOVERNANCE OF THE WTO

The disorganization at Seattle was not only embarrassing and insulting to developing-country delegations; it was also dysfunctional. Excluding most of them from every negotiating session virtually assured opposition to any deal. No provision was made even for effective informal communication. The traditional negotiating rule of the GATT is that negotiating sessions are restricted to thirty participants – chosen from among the largest traders in each sector. Thus some countries attended all sessions; most attended none. This tradition served well in the previous GATT negotiations where it was mainly industrial-country parties to the GATT that were active in the negotiations. Now, with the WTO expanded to 135 members, most of them developing countries, the traditions may have to be altered.

In the pre-conference discussions in Geneva too, developing countries were substantially ignored. On one occasion their contribution to a list of possible topics for discussion was, contrary to all previous practice and diplomatic nicety, excised by the Secretariat, allegedly at the behest of the USA.

It is clear that means have to be found to improve the institutional functioning of the WTO in general, and, in particular, to involve developing countries more effectively without allowing the pressure of numbers to allow the organization to degenerate into a mere talking shop. This clearly involves strengthening developing countries' capacity to deal with WTO issues – mainly, we suggest, in national capitals, where experts can review trade issues in general, rather than in Geneva. Geneva delegations are certainly important for information gathering and transmitting the messages back and forth to the capital. However, the basic and fundamental homework – preparing the negotiating agenda, analysing the likely effects of the agenda on the country's economic and social development – must be done in the national capital. This requires assistance from other international development agencies and coherence among international organizations in building the capacity of developing countries to deal with trade issues.

In the WTO itself a more streamlined governance would be desirable. This could be based on a smaller body with multi-country constituencies (as in the World Bank and IMF Executive Boards[5]) or

[5] In both the World Bank and the IMF, there are 24 Executive Directors in each institution. Five of them are appointed from the USA, Japan, Germany, France and the UK and the rest represent multi-country constituencies. For example, the Executive Director from Belgium in the IMF speaks and votes not only for Belgium itself, but also for other countries including Austria, Belarus, the Czech Republic, Hungary, Kazakhstan, Luxembourg, the Slovak Republic, Slovenia and Turkey. (For more details, see *www.imf.org/* and *www.worldbank.org/*)

revolving membership (as in the US Federal Reserve Board's Open Market Committee[6]). However, given both the high value that governments place on sovereignty and the domestic sensitivity of trade issues, it is plain that such smaller bodies could have only exploratory and preliminary roles. Governments will accept only trade agreements that they have signed themselves (and that, in many cases, have been approved by their legislatures).

The WTO Secretariat might play a more active role than previously, but it must ultimately be seen to remain neutral in negotiations. Moreover, it is developing-country delegations as much as developed-country ones that have kept the Secretariat so closely under the control of members in the past. Thus there will need to be both a broad agreement between members and a much greater sense of tolerance and trust in Geneva before the Secretariat can start to explore and develop initiatives independently as a means of resolving some of the conflicts that a round will throw up.

Governance clearly requires a great deal of careful thought and analysis over the next few

6 In the US, the Federal Reserve Board's Federal Open Market Committee consists of twelve members: the seven members of the Board of Governors of the Federal Reserve System; the president of the Federal Reserve Bank of New York; and the remaining four members rotate annually among the presidents of the eleven other Reserve Banks. (See *www.federalreserve.gov/*)

months. We cannot attempt to resolve the problems here, but conclude with two observations. First, the answer probably lies in creating greater capacity for technical and non-negotiating discussions to map out alternatives and probe the boundaries of feasibility. Straight decision-taking seems likely to remain based on consensus among all members. Second, while there is plainly a case for wide debate on many issues and for hearing the views of many parties, there seems little virtue in allowing non-governmental actors to participate in decision-making or adjudication, nor even, indeed, of allowing them to observe the Council or intergovernmental negotiating sessions. To be sure, publics observe their parliaments at work first-hand, but they never observe their executives.

10 SUMMARY

This paper discusses ways of breaking the Seattle deadlock and incorporating the developing countries more securely into the world trading system, thereby making the next round a truly 'Development Round'. It argues that the best strategy for developing countries is not to resist a round and liberalization but to embrace them and focus them on their development needs. To be plausible in the current circumstances that will need real concessions and contributions from the developed world. Developing countries should approach WTO negotiations with a firm view of their development priorities, and seek to ensure that WTO obligations will assist in the realization of development objectives.

The paper warns the major developed countries what they have to consider if they are serious about repairing the fractures inside the WTO. It emphasizes a realistic recognition that developing the institutions to lock in the advantages of markets requires time, resources and a sensitivity to the environment in which those institutions have to be developed and operate. 'Recognition' calls for resources and assistance from developed countries, while 'sensitivity' requires greater flexibility in the rules parts of the WTO agreements than was shown previously. In addition, given recent events, some measures are needed to reassure developing- country members of the WTO that they have a significant role to play and significant benefits to reap.

Here we present a realistic and balanced ten-point plan for negotiators from developed and developing countries, including significant trade liberalization for both (and from both), along with institutional and rules reforms. It includes the following:

- A broad-based liberalization of trade in agriculture, manufacture and services;
- Give credit for developing countries' unilateral trade liberalization;
- Reinvent special and differential treatment for the 21st century;
- Legally binding technical assistance;
- Honour the agreement on phasing out the MFA;
- Shift issues of labour standards out of the WTO and into the ILO and enhance the capacity and the enforcement mechanism of the ILO;
- Permit environmental trade policy *only* when multilaterally sanctioned by an appropriate multilateral environmental agreement;

- Drop investment and competition policy off the agenda for now;
- Narrow the differences between the USA and the EU;
- Dramatically improve the governance of the WTO.

The recommendations given in this paper are no walkover, however. Indeed, they will require considerable courage. Developing-country policy-makers will have to tackle fundamental institutional problems and confront domestic protectionist interests. Developed-country leaders will need to get over their blind insistence that their own models of policy and institutions are the only acceptable ones. They also need to confront their interest groups in order to make the significant concessions necessary to ensure that in the long run the trading system survives intact and that all countries can benefit from it.

REFERENCES

Anderson, K., Erwidodo and M. Ingco (1999). 'Integrating Agriculture into the WTO: The Next Phase', paper presented at the WTO/World Bank Conference on Developing Countries in a Millennium Round, 20–21 September 1999, Geneva. *www.worldbank.org/research/trade/archive.html/*

Bhagwati, J. (1998). *A Stream of Windows: Unsettling Reflections on Trade, Immigration, and Democracy*, (Cambridge, MA/London: MIT Press).

Chanda, R. (1999). 'Movement of Natural Persons and Trade in Services: Liberalizing Temporary Movement of Labour under the GATS', paper presented at the workshop session 32 in the Global Development Network Conference on Bridging Knowledge and Policy, 6–8 December 1999, Bonn. *www.gdnet.org/bonn99/workshops/sessions32.htm/*

Croome, J. (1998). *The Present Outlook for Trade Negotiations in the World Trade Organization*, World Bank Policy Research Working Paper, No.1992, World Bank, Washington, DC. *www.worldbank.org/research/trade/archive.html/*

Elbehri, A. et al. (1999). 'Agricultural Liberalization in the New Millennium', paper presented at the

World Bank Conference on Agriculture and the New Trade Agenda from a Development Perspective, 1–2 October 1999, Geneva. *www.worldbank.org/research/trade/archive.html/*

Finger, J. M. (1991). 'Development Economics and the GATT', in J. de Melo and A. Sapir (eds), *Trade Theory and Economic Reform* (Oxford: Basil Blackwell), pp. 203–23.

Finger, J. M. and B. Hoekman (1999). 'Developing Countries and a New Trade Round: Lessons from Recent Research', mimeo, the World Bank, Washington, DC.

Finger, J. M. and P. Schuler (1999). 'Implementation of Uruguay Round Commitments: The Development Challenge', paper presented at the WTO/World Bank Conference on Developing Countries in a Millennium Round, 20–21 September 1999, Geneva. *www.worldbank.org/research/trade/archive.html/*

Henderson, D. (1999). *The MAI Affair: A Story and its Lessons* (London: The Royal Institute of International Affairs).

Hertel, T.W., K. Anderson, J.F. Francois, B. Hoekman and W. Martin (1999). 'Agricultural and Non-Agricultural Liberalization in the Millennium Round', paper presented at the World Bank Conference on Agriculture and the New Trade Agenda from a Development Perspective, 1–2 October 1999, Geneva. *www.worldbank.org/research/trade/archive.html/*

Hertel, T. W. and W. Martin (1999). 'Would Developing Countries Gain from Inclusion of Manufactures in the WTO Negotiations?', paper presented at the WTO/World Bank Conference on Developing Countries in a Millennium Round, 20–21 September 1999, Geneva. *www.worldbank.org/research/trade/archive.html/*

Hoekman, B. (1996). 'Assessing the General Agreement on Trade in Services', Chapter 4 of Martin and Winters (1996), pp. 88–124.

Hoekman, B. and P. Holmes (1999). *Competition Policy, Developing Countries and the World Trade Organization*, Policy Research Working Papers, No. 2211, World Bank, Washington, DC. *www.worldbank.org/research/trade/archive.html*

Krueger, A.O. (1999). *Developing Countries and the next Round of Multilateral Trade Negotiations*, Policy Research Working Papers, No. 2118, World Bank, Washington, DC. *www.worldbank.org/research/trade/archive.html/*

Martin, W. and Francois, J. (1994). 'Bindings and Rules as Trade Liberalization', in A. Deardorff (ed.), *Quiet Pioneering: Robert M. Stern and his International Economic Legacy* (Ann Arbor, MI: University of Michigan).

Martin, W. and L. A. Winters (1996). *The Uruguay Round and the Developing Countries* (Cambridge: Cambridge University Press).

Mattoo, A. (1999). 'Developing Countries in the New Round of GATS Negotiations: From a Defensive to a Pro-active Role', paper presented at the WTO/ World Bank Conference on Developing Countries in a Millennium Round, 20–21 September 1999, Geneva. *www.worldbank.org/research/trade/ archive.html/*

Ravallion, M. and G. Datt (1996). 'How Important to India's Poor is the Sectoral Composition of Economic Growth?', *World Bank Economic Review*, Vol.10, pp.1–25.

Rollo, J. and L. A. Winters (2000). 'Subsidiarity and Governance Challenges for the WTO: The Examples of Environmental and Labour Standards', forthcoming in *The World Economy.*

Short, C. (1999). 'Making the Next Trade Round Work for the World's Poor', speech by Clare Short, UK Secretary of State for International Development, hosted by the Commonwealth Business Council at the Hatton Conference Centre, London, 3 November 1999.

Tyers, R. and R. Falvey (1989). 'Border Price Changes and Domestic Welfare in the Presence of Subsidised Exports', *Oxford Economic Papers*, Vol. 41, pp. 434–51.

Wang, Z.K. and L. A. Winters (1997). 'Africa's Role in Multilateral Trade Negotiations: Past and Future', *Journal of African Economies*, Vol. 7, Supplement 1.

Whalley, J. (1999). 'Special and Differential Treatment in the Millennium Round', *The World Economy*, Vol. 22, No. 8, 1065–93.

Winters, L. A. (1991) *International Economics* (London: Routledge, 4th edn).

World Bank (1999). Papers presented at the WTO/ World Bank Conference on Developing Countries in a Millennium Round, 20–21 September 1999, Geneva, can also be obtained at the World Bank International Trade and Development website, *www1.worldbank.org/wbiep/trade/* They are also forthcoming in *The World Economy*.

By the same authors:

COHERENCE IN INTERNATIONAL ECONOMIC POLICY-MAKING

ZHEN KUN WANG AND L. ALAN WINTERS

The issue of coherence among international organizations has attracted considerable attention, particularly since the birth of the WTO. The Uruguay Round Declaration recognized the role of trade liberalization in achieving greater coherence in global economic policy-making, stating that the WTO shall cooperate with the IMF and the World Bank. This paper explores the origins of the concept of coherence, its evolution after the Uruguay Round, the history and outcome of negotiations among international organizations, ways in which these bodies can work together, and what coherence should imply from both a general trade policy perspective and a development point of view.